>> CODE POWER: A TEEN PROGRAMMER'S GUIDE ™

GETTING TO KNOW

Scratch

JEANNE NAGLE

rosen publishing's
rosen
central®

NEW YORK

Published in 2015 by The Rosen Publishing Group, Inc.
29 East 21st Street, New York, NY 10010

Library of Congress Cataloging-in-Publication Data

Nagle, Jeanne, author.
Getting to know Scratch/Jeanne Nagle.—First edition.
     pages cm.—(Code power: a teen programmer's guide)
Audience: Grades 5 to 8.
Includes bibliographical references and index.
ISBN 978-1-4777-7697-1 (library bound) — ISBN 978-1-4777-7699-5 (pbk.) — ISBN 978-1-4777-7700-8 (6-pack)
1. Scratch (Computer program language)—Juvenile literature. 2. Computer programming—Juvenile literature. I. Title.
QA76.7.N345 2015
005.13'3—dc23

                                        2013045601

Manufactured in the United States of America

{CONTENTS

S tudents all over the world are taught languages other than the one they grew up speaking. Many are learning a foreign language at a young age. Most schools in countries belonging to the European Union teach English beginning in the elementary grades. North American countries, including the United States, offer classes in second languages such as Spanish and French.

Yet there is one type of language that for years was taught only in high school or, more likely, college or universities—and only then to particular groups of students. In the past, computer languages were learned primarily by older students who had decided to work as computer programmers or in a related field. These languages were very complicated to learn and were written in code that depended on extra-careful attention to detail. One little mistake in the code and all meaning was lost.

Researchers and education experts have found ways to simplify the process of learning computer languages. Because of these breakthroughs, elementary and middle school students are able to write computer programs, too. They create their own games, music videos, interactive stories, and much more. Beyond

UCTION

fun and games, simplified computer programming also teaches students skills such as math, logic, and problem solving.

One of the most popular new computer languages is Scratch. Introduced in 2007, Scratch improved upon an earlier computer

Middle school students are now able to learn programming techniques, thanks to simplified languages such as Scratch.

language called Logo, which was popular in the 1970s and '80s. Using Logo, people could create designs by drawing basic shapes using a cursor that was shaped like a turtle. Logo itself was a simplified way to program computers because it added "natural language," meaning terms and phrases that users would commonly write or speak, in its commands. Before Logo, computer programming was done using code, which looked more like strings of numbers and symbols than a language the average person could read and understand.

Scratch eliminates the need to master complicated code by packaging commands into colorful blocks that users drag and drop onto an on-screen workspace. Block by block users build a program, less concerned about syntax, which involves the rules surrounding how code should be written, and better able to concentrate on the logic behind their creations.

All computer languages have the same goal: to let users "talk" to computers in order to make the machines do work for them. Using blocks of ready-made code in a simple drag-and-drop format, Scratch has made translating from computer command to on-screen action so much easier.

CHAPTER 1

STARTING FROM SCRATCH

The expression "from scratch" refers to the creation of something unique using only basic parts or ingredients, starting from the very beginning. In order to learn about the Scratch computer language, it makes sense to start at the very beginning, when the language was first developed. To truly get to know Scratch, however, it is best to go a little further back than that, to discuss similar programming languages that came before.

KIDS LEARNING CODE

For many years, there has been interest in teaching students, even those in grade school, how to write computer code. In the 1970s and '80s, personal computers were gaining popularity. As more children started using computers at home and in schools, educators thought it would be a good idea if the youngsters weren't simply passive users. Playing games or doing basic word processing wasn't enough. Teachers wanted students to become programmers as a way to increase knowledge not only of computers but also of mathematics and logic. Both math and logic are required to write computer programs.

A magazine cover from the 1970s promotes what was then a new product, the home computer.

The types of programming languages in existence at the time, such as BASIC and Pascal, were very complicated. The level of math and logic used to write code in these languages was quite advanced. Only people who had studied computer science in college and had experience writing code were able to program computers easily using these languages.

The problem with children learning computer programming was that writing code required skills that school-age kids did not have. For instance, in grade school, students learn how the language they speak and write is put together to form proper sentences. This is called syntax. Educators decided that learning the syntax of one of the existing computer programming languages, which were much different from that of a person's spoken language, would be too difficult for younger students. So researchers started working on ways to make programming easier for young minds.

THE ARRIVAL OF LOGO

In 1967, a team from the Massachusetts Institute of Technology (MIT) Artificial Intelligence Laboratory developed a simpler computer language called Logo. Based on an advanced programming language called Lisp, Logo was first used on large computers called mainframes. Users keyed in commands to make a robotic turtle move across the floor. When smaller personal computers began to be used in homes and schools in the 1970s, Logo moved the action onto the computer screen, using a turtle-shaped icon to draw shapes and designs. The process was still the same, with users keying commands to make the on-screen turtle move.

Logo kept undergoing changes over the years. Computer scientists were trying to make the programming language better and even easier to use. In the 1990s, they came up with a new version called Logo Blocks. Users no longer had to key in commands but instead built programs using prewritten chunks, or blocks, of code. This version of Logo was the basis for the development of the Scratch programming language.

AND THEN THERE WAS SCRATCH

As with Logo, the story of Scratch begins at MIT, in the university's Media Lab. Researchers in the lab's Lifelong Kindergarten group were looking for creative ways to use digital technology. In 2003, they began work on the Scratch computer programming language. Researchers at the University of California–Los Angeles (UCLA) also worked on the project, which was funded by the National Science

Foundation (NSF) and the computer-technology company Intel. The first version of Scratch software, which was designed with

This aerial view of the Cambridge and Boston area shows the MIT campus. MIT is a highly respected school for students interested in science, engineering, economics, and other fields.

users age eight through fifteen in mind, was introduced to the public in 2007. Later versions of the software were developed with the help of computer and technology companies such as Microsoft, Samsung, and Motorola.

What makes Scratch different from traditional programming languages is that it uses a graphical interface, rather than strings of written code. To understand what the term "graphical interface" means, simply take the words apart and define them. "Graphical" refers to graphics, which are pictures and shapes. "Interface" is another way to describe when two things—in this case, a computer and a user—connect or otherwise communicate with each other to create action. Today's computers typically use graphical interfaces to perform many tasks.

The key to Scratch is programming blocks, which are a lot like Logo Blocks. Instead of keying in strings of complicated code, users choose from a menu of ready-made commands that are placed inside of graphics that, on a computer screen, look like blocks that come in various colors. Each color represents a different menu item, such as "Motion" or "Sound." Using their computer's cursor, users drag and drop blocks to an on-screen work area, called a canvas, connecting them as they go along. The blocks have indentations and tabs, like puzzle pieces, so each block will connect only with certain other blocks. That way, there is less of a chance that beginners will make mistakes in their programming.

The original version of Scratch was the result of years of research. Testing the software while it was still being developed was the job of teens who were part of computer giant Intel's Computer Clubhouse—an international network of

>> PROGRAMMABLE BRICKS

One inspiration for Scratch was a simple toy that children had been playing with for years—Lego building blocks. Blocks of Scratch code are designed to snap together like the popular toy blocks. Adult researchers have also played with Legos, not just for fun but to advance the field of robotics using microcomputers.

In the 1990s, MIT researchers found a way to transfer programming information to a tiny computer built into a Lego brick. These programmable bricks, as they were called, could communicate through sensors to machines or robots built with Lego blocks, motors, and gears.

MIT has designed and created several versions of the programmable brick. As of 2013, the latest version is called the Cricket. Working with MIT and "inspired" by the university's research, Lego created its own version of a programmable block, the RCX, in 1998. Lego's latest version is the NXT. The Lego programmable bricks operate the company's Mindstorms robotics kits.

adult-supervised clubs where kids learn through using computers and other technology. The creators of Scratch also got feedback from children in U.S. classrooms where the software was tested.

FLOORS, CEILINGS, AND WALLS

Development of Scratch was heavily influenced by the work of Seymour Papert, the MIT professor who cofounded the university's Media Lab and is credited with inventing the Logo

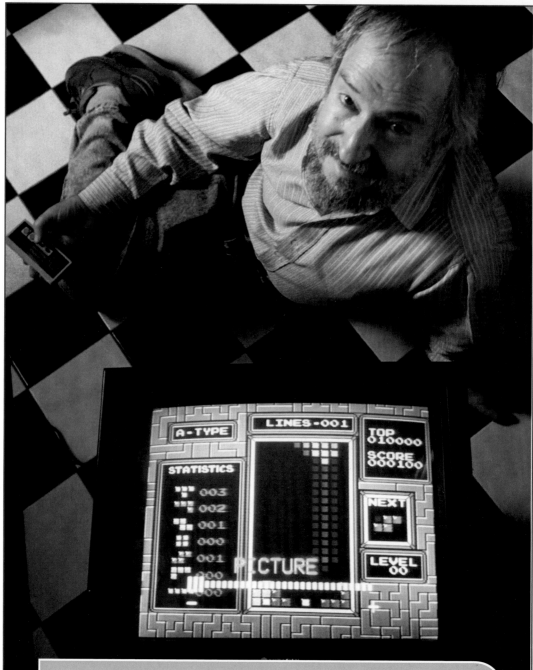

Computer education expert Seymour Papert, sitting on the floor with a computer game, in the 1990s. Papert's work was highly influential in the creation of Scratch.

programming language. Papert believed that computers in the classroom were powerful learning tools but that they had to be used properly. Children were simply passive users of technology, he argued, when they needed to take a more active role through behaviors such as programming. The trouble was that programming was (and is) difficult and tricky even for adults to learn, let alone young children.

Papert came up with an approach to creating computer languages that can be likened to building a room. He said any programming language designed for children should have a "low floor," meaning entry should be easy and accessible to everyone. Furthermore, there should be "high ceilings" so that there would be room for more tools and information to be built up later on, and "wide walls," which could hold the work of many people from all sorts of backgrounds and education levels. In order for kids and other beginners to be able to program computers, the approach would have to be easy, expandable, and capable of great diversity.

Mitchel Resnick, the MIT professor who led the team that developed Scratch, was a student of Papert's at the university. He incorporated many of Papert's concepts into the creation of the computer language he built for children. Resnick has said that Scratch has a low floor, where practically anyone can create a new project or open and investigate someone else's work. He added that projects with lots of action and many graphics and characters are welcome, thanks to the software's high ceilings, and the walls are sufficiently wide enough to "incorporate music, sound, and digital images, and can be designed to be interactive."

SHOOTING FOR THE GOALS

Beyond designing around floors, ceilings, and walls, the creative team behind Scratch also decided early on that they wanted their software to achieve three goals, which they called design principles. These are "tinkerability," meaningfulness, and sociability.

The first principle refers to a design that encourages students to tinker, or experiment, with the software and not feel hemmed-in by a structure that is too rigid or unforgiving of mistakes that beginners are bound to make.

Resnick has stated that Scratch was designed so that user projects would be "personally meaningful." The variety of projects that can be created using Scratch means that people can work on what interests them. Further, the software gives users the ability to showcase personal items in their projects, such as their own photos, music that they like, and even their own recorded voices. In other words, each user's personality shines through using Scratch.

As for sociability, Scratch was designed with the idea of having users share their finished projects with an online community. The Scratch Web site not only lets users post their projects but also gives them the opportunity to tinker with, or remix, the work of other Scratchers.

The larger goal behind all of these design elements was to create a programming environment that was easy for kids to use. Looking at the numbers, it's safe to assume that Scratch has succeeded on that front. As of fall 2013, more than two million people have become registered users of the software, sharing nearly four million projects on the Scratch Community Web site.

>> HIP-HOP INSPIRATION

Tinkering is at the very heart of Scratch, so much so that it was even the inspiration for the software's name. Hip-hop disc jockeys practice the art of "scratching," which involves manipulating existing recorded material and mixing sounds to create a unique audio product. The folks at MIT decided that their software was the programming equivalent of scratching. Beginning programmers are like DJs, mixing together graphics, animation, photos, sound, and music to create projects that are as individual as the users themselves.

FREE AND EASY

When Scratch was first introduced to the public, anybody could download the software from the Scratch site for free. All users have to do to obtain version 2.0, unveiled in 2013, is browse through the cloud—again, at no cost. MIT has made Scratch open-source software, which means that there are no licenses or costs associated with using it.

Being open-source makes sense for Scratch, since simply downloading or connecting via the Internet is arguably the easiest way to obtain software. "Easy" has been a keyword behind the development of Scratch right from the beginning.

CHAPTER 2

THE NUTS AND BOLTS OF SCRATCH

T he Lifelong Kindergarten team at MIT began work on Scratch in 2003 but didn't release it until 2007. Development took four years, and even then the team was still making improvements and working out the bugs. Launching a visual programming environment like Scratch takes time because there are so many issues to consider. That is the nature of programming. Writing code, considering all the options, anticipating problems, and structuring statements, or commands, in such a way that they'll make sense when put into action is a painstaking process.

The irony is that all this time and work went into making a product that was simple to use. The idea behind Scratch is that all the elements that go into programming are reduced to their simplest form. It is kind of like baking a cake using a mix, where a bunch of ingredients are already put together; just add water, oil, and eggs, and bake. The team at MIT has gathered together programming elements, most notably coding and a logic structure, for programmers to use as a base. All users need to do then is add their own elements—sound, pictures, and most

Individuals are free to add their own creative elements to projects undertaken using Scratch programming software.

important, their creativity—to those "bundled" by the software's creators and their project comes out fully formed and functional.

Following is a brief overview of how Scratch works, from the various elements the creators used to the basic ways in which the software works.

FIRST THINGS FIRST

Upon opening Scratch, users encounter the user interface, which is a window that has several panes, or palettes. The original Scratch, which left off at version 1.4, had a slightly different layout of the interface than version 2.0 and beyond, but each version (Scratch 1.x and Scratch 2.x, with the "x" referring to subversions of the software) contains the same four basic panels.

To the left in version 1.4 is the block palette, which contains the categories of Scratch blocks divided by method, or action.

>> BEING OBJECTIVE

In programming, a collection of data, or information, stored in a computer's memory is called an object. The data is transformed into something recognizable that appears on the computer screen, such as an animated character, a tree, a bird in the tree, etc. Even the backdrop or setting against which other objects appear is considered an object in the world of programming.

Scratch is an object-oriented programming environment, which means it puts the focus on the objects and the actions they perform in a project. The Lifelong Kindergarten group designed the software this way because object orientation is very visual, meaning it is easy for beginners to see what the programs they build can do. If the objects on-screen do not behave as the programmer wanted or expected them to, he or she can simply go back and fix the error by changing a block of code.

In programming, a method is a statement that tells objects on a computer screen how to act. Methods allow programmers to change how an on-screen object looks, moves, sounds, etc. The block palette appears as a strip panel in the middle of the interface in version 2.0.

In version 1.4 of Scratch, to the immediate right of the command block panel is a space that is called the script panel. This is the area into which command blocks are dragged and dropped as users build their projects. In Scratch 2.0, the script panel is to the far right of the interface window.

The panel in the upper-right corner of the window in version 1.4, and to the upper left in version 2.0, is referred to as the stage. This is where users can run and view their projects. The animated cat that is part of the Scratch logo appears in the stage panel when users start a new project. He is easily deleted so that users can add objects that suit the purposes of their own projects.

Finally, the last panel within the larger window is where users can choose objects to populate their projects. In Scratch, objects are called sprites. The list of sprites appears underneath the stage in both versions of Scratch.

PLAYING WITH BLOCKS

Programmers in MIT's Media Lab had already completed work on the Logo programming language and the robot-construction kit Lego Mindstorms before releasing Scratch. The visual programming environment borrowed heavily from the others, particularly when it came to programming and language concepts. While those first two projects were no doubt influential, perhaps

The new home of the MIT Media Lab and the Lifelong Kindergarten group, which opened its doors in 2010.

the greatest inspiration for the development of Scratch came from actual Lego bricks themselves. Instead of building castles or race cars out of physical interlocking blocks made out of plastic resin, Scratch users were meant to build computer projects by virtually snapping together graphical blocks that contain prewritten code.

Scratch blocks come in different shapes, which determine the ways in which they can be connected to other blocks. The most common type of Scratch blocks are called, appropriately enough, stack blocks. They are shaped like simple rectangles with notches on top and bumps, or indentations, on the bottom—much like Lego bricks that have top "studs" and hollow "tubes" underneath. The majority of stack blocks are command blocks, meaning they contain statements that tell the animated objects how to behave on-screen when the program is run. Others are shaped like the letter "C," which are generally control blocks. These are like stacked command blocks, but they also wrap around other blocks in order to control certain behaviors, such as repeating a command.

Each category of block is also represented in a specific color. For instance, motion command blocks are dark blue, while commands that determine how an object looks are purple.

As of the release of the beta version of Scratch 2.0 in January 2013, users were able to create their own blocks.

WRITING THE SCRIPT

Movies and plays begin with a script, which is a written document that contains information about characters, storyline, and dialogue. A script in programming terms is quite similar. Instead of written words on a page, though, programming scripts consist of line upon line of code that controls what characters are part of a project, as well as what the characters do and say. Scratch scripts are a little different still. Instead of lots of code, Scratch scripts are made up of several colorful command blocks snapped together and stacked like a coding totem pole.

Each script in Scratch begins with what is known as a "hat block." Also called an event block, a hat block is a command block with a rounded top that has no indentation. Without an indentation, no other block can snap onto the top of a hat block.

NOW APPEARING ONSTAGE

When first opening the Scratch interface, the stage is a blank space on which all of the project's action will take place. In the course of creating a project, however, the stage does not stay blank for long. Backdrops can be added to the stage to give a project more color and depth.

When users click on the "stage" icon, found in the sprite panel of the interface, a "backdrops" tab appears in the script panel. Clicking on that tab gives users the option to "paint" (create) their own backdrop, or import a colorful background scene from a menu of backdrops that have already been created by the Scratch team. Imported backdrops are categorized as indoors, outdoors, nature, and sports.

MAKE PROJECTS, NOT MISCHIEF

By definition, sprites are supernatural characters that resemble elves or pixies, which are described as mischievous. In Scratch, a sprite is any object used in a project—including one of the most popular characters in the Scratch programming environment, an odd little elf-like creature known as Gobo. Rather than pulling pranks and causing trouble, however, Scratch character sprites—such as Gobo and his friends Pico, Nano, Giga, and Terra—are more likely to be called cute or charming.

Scratch has a library full of sprites available for use in projects, divided by category, theme, and type (bitmap or vector). Most are drawn as simple cartoon characters, but there are also a number of photographic images of people, animals, modes of transportation, and things (props, if you will). The fifth category of sprites, fantasy, contains only drawn characters, but it is the home of the popular Gobo and friends.

For beginning programmers who are a bit more adventurous, there is an icon that, when clicked, calls up an art palette that lets them "paint" their own sprites. Also, sprites may be uploaded from a computer file or created by taking a picture using the programmer's webcam.

While Scratch can be taught in computer labs, the language is so easy to use that students can also figure it out as they create animations.

Whereas blocks are dragged and dropped onto the script palette, sprites are dragged onto the stage and dropped directly into the action. Sprites being used in a particular project stay visible as thumbnail images in the sidebar panel. Clicking on a sprite's thumbnail gives users the ability to view and edit that sprite's scripts, sounds, and costumes, which is what the different versions of the same sprite in various poses or "moods" are called.

SPEAKING THE LANGUAGE

It's not just the easy drag-and-drop functionality of Scratch that makes it such a good programming environment for novices. In traditional coding, users must place a lot of letters, numbers, and punctuation marks in the exact right order for a program to run smoothly, or even run at all. This can be a time-consuming and frustrating experience for someone who is not experienced in such an activity. Having code packed into the boxes lets children and other beginners concentrate on building programs, rather than keying in complicated coding themselves.

>> APPLE A DAY KEEPS SCRATCH AWAY

Data compiled by MDG Advertising confirms what many people have known for a while—Apple's iPad tablet is a huge hit with kids. Because it's fun and easy to use, Scratch is pretty popular with the younger set as well. It would seem like using Scratch on the iPad would be a natural, blockbuster pairing.

So why was a Scratch viewer app, written by an independent programmer specifically for use on the iPad and the iPhone, yanked from the Apple Store in April 2010?

Many critics of the decision seemed to think that Apple's policydisallowing the use of code-interpreting apps, such as Java or AdobeFlash, on the iPhone was to blame. The policy is in place toprevent apps from running executable code that has not been approved

The decision by Apple not to carry the viewing app created quite an uproar in the computing and education communities. Apple promised to reconsider the company's decision not to carry the app, but as of fall 2013, the app has not been reinstated.

"I'm disappointed that Apple decided not to allow a Scratch player on the iPhone or iPad," Scratch creator Mitch Resnick stated in an e-mail message at the time. "In my mind, there is nothing more important than empowering the next generation of kids to design, create, and express themselves with new media technologies. I hope that Apple will reconsider its policies so that more kids can experience the joys of creating and sharing with Scratch. Our group is planning to make Scratch authoring tools for the iPad in the future, and we hope Apple will allow us."

Scratch is written in a computer language called Squeak, which is a dialect of another programming language called Small talk. Originally part of a project conducted by researchers at Apple Computer, Squeak is open source and an early example of object-oriented programming languages.

ALL SYSTEMS GO

Scratch is designed to run on PCs and Macs, desktops and laptops, and is compatible with Windows XP, Vista, and 7; Mac OSX, version 10.4 and later; and Linux operating systems. Versions 1 through 1.4 of the open-source software were downloadable. Version 1.4 required a display of 800 x 480 or larger, and at least 120 megabytes of free disk space to accommodate the download.

A newer edition of Scratch, version 2.0 is based on Adobe Flash and requires that a computer have version 10.2 or later installed to run. Other requirements include a fairly recent Web browser—evidence suggests that Scratch works best with Safari and Chrome—and a display of at least 1,024 x 768. Another crucial change is that Scratch 2.0 operates in the cloud, meaning users can work in the programming environment right in their browser, no downloading necessary. By making this move, Scratch opened itself up to becoming available to an even wider audience, including users of Chromebooks and other tech devices designed to store data and apps in the cloud.

CHAPTER 3

SCRATCHING A CREATIVE ITCH

At a presentation during the 2012 TED (Technology, Entertainment, Design) conference, Scratch creator Mitch Resnick recounted how, during the previous May, he had gone on the Scratch Web site to see how many kids had decided to use the software to create Mother's Day cards. Resnick was "surprised and delighted to see a list of dozens and dozens" of interactive cards created by young Scratch users and shared with the Scratch community. So instead of creating his own card to send to his mother, which was the original reason he had visited the site to begin with, he wound up sending his mom links to a bunch of other people's cards.

This story illustrates just one of the inventive ways—interactive greeting cards—Scratch users have put the software to good use. It also highlights another interesting point. Resnick, who is in his fifties, was on the site to make a Mother's Day card, just like all the middle and high schoolers whose cards he did end up sharing with his mom. So although Scratch was designed for kids, there is no age limit as to who participates—or creative limit on why they would use it.

Creating greeting cards with a personal flair, as this young woman is doing, is just one of the activities attempted by beginning programmers using Scratch.

HITTING (AND OVERSHOOTING) THE TARGET

The Lifelong Kindergarten team at MIT created Scratch to help children get a head start in computer programming, or at the very least help them learn that there was more to computing than using programs that emphasized a more passive use of technology. With that in mind, they developed a computer programming environment aimed at a target audience of eight to sixteen years old.

>> ONE USER'S EXPERIENCE

Ray was eight years old and shadowing his programmer dad at a "take your kids to work" event when he first used Scratch. As a teenager, he looked back on the experience.

How easy was Scratch to use and learn?

It took a bit to get started, but after that it was intuitive.

How did it compare to other programming software you may have used?

It is similar to other beginner's programming languages, such as Lego Mindstorms NXT, but not as much as, for instance, the programs for the FIRST Robotics Competition Robots, which are more text intensive.

What have you created using Scratch?

The biggest example that comes to mind is a primitive painting program that I call Etch-A-Sketch 2.0. It improves on the classic toy in three major ways. The first is that you can insert gaps into the lines, the second is that you can use multiple different colors, and the third is that you can move the pointer to the center and/or make it follow the cursor.

Why did you choose not to share your creations on the Scratch Web site?

I didn't post my programs on the Web site for two main reasons. The first is that I have only recently been allowed to post things on the Web, and the second is that I am still working out bugs and adding more features to the ones that I wanted to post the most (with my parent's permission, of course).

What's your favorite part about using Scratch?

It is significantly more intuitive than any other programming language that I have used (chiefly the Lego Mindstorms NXT programming language), the fact that I can edit the sprites of any of the objects in the program in the developer itself, and that I don't need to create or download a class library.

Would you recommend Scratch to others who are interested in learning programming?

I would wholeheartedly advise anyone who wants to start programming to at least give Scratch a try. Even though it has its differences from major programming languages (for example, Basic, C, Java, and C++), it shares many of the same elements and helps you to be able to think like a computer just following instructions, not like a human who knows to look ahead.

In the years since Scratch was first launched, something that was somewhat unexpected, yet entirely welcome, happened. The team at MIT noticed that the target age range for the software was expanding, particularly within the upper age ranges. Sixteen was no longer the cutoff age. College students and adults, many of whom had little to no experience with computer programming, were turning to Scratch as a way to learn and have fun while being creative.

Part of the reason for this expansion in user age was due to an adaptation to the ways in which the software was being used. Originally designed to be pretty much self-directed, meaning users were supposed to take it upon themselves to "play around" in the program's interface with minimal formal supervision, Scratch was starting to be used in middle and high school classrooms. Even some colleges were using Scratch to help illustrate principles behind programming in the beginning computer science classes.

RICH IN CREATIVITY

One reason Scratch is so popular is that it puts the power of programming into the hands of amateur users. The software also gives people an easy and fun way to express themselves. Scratch is an example of a rich media environment, meaning there are several different elements that users can incorporate into their projects: objects, sound, photographs, video, graphics, text, animation, and interactivity.

Essentially, Scratch users can let their imaginations run wild when creating projects, the scripts for which can be as simple or detailed as they want. To get the creative juices flowing, the Lifelong Kindergarten team at MIT has helpfully offered what they call "Starter Projects," bare-bones projects that come with suggestions regarding how users might change or "remix" them to make their own. (The term "remix" is another nod to the disc jockey analogy that gave Scratch its name.) The starter projects are divided into six popular categories:

- **Animation**—Users can customize an animated greeting card, have sprites interact as part of a talk show hosted by Pico, or place a virtual version of themselves in the middle of the floor at a dance party.

- **Games**—Versions of one of the world's first video games, *Pong*, and a classic maze join electronic hide-and-seek and sprite dress-up as starter games.
- **Interactive Art**—These starters are a case of art meeting computer programming. Clicking on a computer's mouse, space bar, or arrow keys lets users "paint" designs, amplify sound, or make a wizard cast a variety of spells on a dragon.
- **Music and Dance**—Arrow keys dictate the moves of two "street" dancers, while a mouse-click brings the keys of an animated piano to life. The Scratch cat even plays disc jockey in one of the starter projects in this category.
- **Stories**—The "once upon a time" beginning of a castle adventure and the chance to share a "random" mini-autobiography are two of the stories started by Scratch creators that users can bring to "The End." Also in this category are a sprite profile and a virtual tour of the Lifelong Kindergarten offices at MIT.
- **Video Sensing**—After asking permission to access a computer's webcam and microphone, Scratch incorporates a real-time video image of the user into an on-screen activity that requires him or her to move to complete a task. Popping on-screen bubbles, musical notes, tossing pizza dough, and saving Lego-like figures from falling into an animated sea are the starter projects that users can customize in this category.

There's no need for antiquated joysticks, used in the original *Pong* game by Atari. Scratch can create a "starter" version of the game that is controlled by computer keystrokes.

>> STUDENTS TEACHING TEACHERS

All that the members of a girls' STEAM (Science, Technology, Engineering, Arts, Math) club in South Fayette, Pennsylvania, expected to do was show off Scratch projects they had created at a regional technology conference. But sharing their enthusiasm for the programming software didn't stop there. In short order, the girls were teaching visitors at a community learning night how to use Scratch. Within two years Scratch had been introduced as an educational tool throughout the South Fayette school district—and students were once again taking the lead as instructors in the software's use.

The STEAM club girls have not been the only young scholars who have taken an active role in the spread of Scratch as a teaching tool in South Fayette. After presenting at the opening of TransformED—a space where teachers from forty-two school districts across Pennsylvania come to experiment with new learning technology—students from South Fayette Middle School traveled to a nearby town to train teachers in that town's school district how to use Scratch.

Adults seem to approve of the students' collective efforts. When he came to speak at the University of Pittsburgh, Mitch Resnick met briefly with a dozen or so South Fayette middle and high school students who had been invited to serve as instructors at a STEAM summer session for area teachers. These same students have considered sharing their Scratch knowledge with other groups, such as Girl Scout troops.

"Having students involved on a leadership level allows us to expand our opportunities to more students in ways we could not before," said Aileen Owens, South Fayette school district's director of technology and innovation.

SCRATCHING UP INTEREST IN SCHOOLS

In an interview that appeared on the official TED blog, Mitch Resnick talked about the value of students learning programming

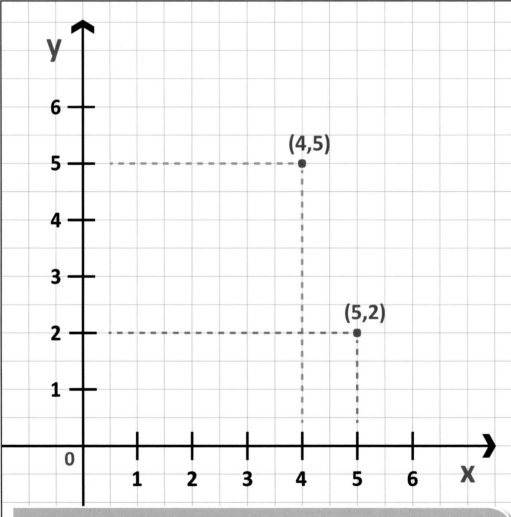

This is an example of a Cartesian system graph. Scratch uses this type of coordinate system to help place sprites where programmers want them to appear within an animation.

at an early age within the school system. "When you learn to read, you can then read to learn," he was quoted as saying. "And it's the same thing with coding. If you learn to code, you can code to learn."

Even though Scratch was originally designed so that users did not need help or outside instruction, the software has been increasingly used as an educational tool, particularly in classrooms across the United States and the United Kingdom. Educators are finding ways to incorporate Scratch projects into their curriculums in an attempt to make learning fun.

First, there is the obvious use of Scratch to teach computer programming skills. There is a movement afoot to teach elementary and middle school students more than basic user skills on the computer. Members of the movement, including Scratch developer Mitch Resnick, believe that kids should learn more about computers than what they call "Office" skills, referencing the word processing and spreadsheet programs that come packaged in Microsoft's Office software. Those kinds of user skills are great, they argue, but teaching children how to create programs lets them see how computers work, thereby providing them with useful skills in a world that relies on computers more and more for basic tasks.

Scratch also helps strengthen students' math skills. A number of the programming blocks contain areas that users fill in with values and variables, which are fundamental math concepts. Students gain experience with the Cartesian coordinate system, which involves plotting points on a graph, when they place sprites on the Scratch stage—although most likely they don't even realize that this is what they're learning. Drawing geometrical shapes is part math project and part art. Additionally, students can create their own simple math games using Scratch or play with any of the many existing games posted on the math projects Web site.

Along the same lines as the math projects page, a few projects that help teach word identification and reading to preschoolers also reside on the Scratch Web site. Older students, however, will be able to hone their language skills by writing short stories, which they can illustrate themselves using Scratch.

Beyond helping to teach specific subject matter within the curriculum, using Scratch also imparts practical life skills. According to Resnick, these include creative thinking, logic, systematic reasoning, and working collaboratively. Other educators point out that building Scratch projects also gives kids experience prioritizing tasks and planning to ensure a smooth workflow.

CHAPTER 4

SCRATCHING EACH OTHER'S BACKS

The Lifelong Kindergarten team developed Scratch so that various elements could be mixed together to form interesting media-rich projects. More than that, though, the software was designed so that the projects of one user could be "remixed" with the work of others, creating entirely new projects cobbled together from the best elements of many works. The development team believes that this spirit of collaboration is a big part of what makes Scratch so popular with users, who become part of an online community of "Scratchers" as soon as they register and post projects.

Project sharing is built into the software through various studios on the Scratch site. In the physical world, a sense of community and collaboration can be found via a number of clubs that have formed around using the software.

WELCOME TO THE SCRATCH COMMUNITY

The Lifelong Kindergarten group takes the concept of "community" very seriously. The group takes the term to mean a group of people who not only are banded together by common interests or goals—in this case, the common factor being the use of Scratch software to learn computer programming—but who also communicate, collaborate, and share ideas and resources. In other words, it's not enough simply to have commonality. To be part of the Scratch community, users must choose to be active members who share what they have (their projects and ideas) with others. They also agree to abide by certain rules.

>> THE GUIDE TO BEING A GOOD SCRATCHER

Sharing is such an important part of Scratch that the concept is reinforced by appearing in the Scratch Community Guidelines. But that's not all it takes to be a member in good standing within the community. Scratch developers have posted some commonsense rules about behavior while working on the Scratch site—rules that would serve users well in an offline community such as school or business, too:

- **Be respectful.** When sharing projects or posting comments, remember that people of many different ages and backgrounds will see what you've shared.

- **Be constructive.** When commenting on others' projects, say something you like about it and offer suggestions.
- **Share.** You are free to remix projects, ideas, images, or anything else you find on Scratch—and anyone can use anything that you share. Be sure to give credit when you remix.
- **Keep personal info private.** For safety reasons, don't use real names or post contact information like phone numbers or addresses.
- **Help keep the site friendly.** If you think a project or comment is mean, insulting, violent, or otherwise inappropriate, click "Report" to report it.

Users must register on the Scratch site to become part of the online community. Registration is free and involves sharing some basic information, such as gender, country, birth month and year, and a contact e-mail address. Members make up a username and create a password so that they can log in as registered users. The online registration form also asks for city and state, but this is not required information.

The benefits of being a registered member of the Scratch community are simple, and they revolve around sharing projects. Unregistered users are free to experiment in Scratch, and they can view and run projects created by others. But only registered users can download projects for remixing or comment on the work of other members. Users must also be registered to tag their projects. Tagging, or attaching key words, to a project

Though they may seem to be working alone at a computer, Scratch users are actually part of a larger online community that works together to create projects.

helps bring it to the attention of other users who are seeking a specific kind of work to view and/or remix. Registered members of the Scratch community also have an unlimited number of project uploads and can create their own studios.

ARTISTS IN VIRTUAL RESIDENCE

Artists of all kinds conduct their work in what is known as a studio. This is a space where painters, sculptors, dancers, photographers, writers, and actors are free to create. Since the users of Scratch can be considered "programming artists," who create projects that combine several forms of artistic media (music, images, text), the software developers gave them studio space on the Scratch Web site to create and share their work.

Formerly known as galleries in Scratch 1.x, studios can be accessed by members and nonmembers alike. There are four tabs in the studio interface: projects, comments, curators, and activity. The projects tab automatically opens when members enter a studio, revealing thumbnails of various projects created by the member who built the studio, who is called the curator.

Although the studio curator is identified when the studio is entered, users can also find out more about the studio owner by clicking on the curator tab, then clicking on the hyperlink of the curator's name. This takes users to an expanded studio page,

>> COMMONLY CREATIVE

Although there is an emphasis on sharing, Scratch also has a way to protect the creative rights of its members. Uploaded projects fall under the protection of a license provided by the nonprofit organization Creative Commons. Unlike a copyright, which reserves all rights for a creative work's originator, Creative Commons licenses are tailored to reserve only those rights needed in each individual case.

The license used by Scratch states that remixers must attribute their work to the creator of the original project. What's more, when they post their remix, they have to leave their work open to the same treatment; any remixed work has to be available to a remix as well.

Additionally, as every project is uploaded, it is embedded with an attribution code, which identifies its creator. Attribution gives credit where credit is due—with the creator of the original project, who retains ownership of his or her work.

where curators can add information about who they are, what projects they're working on, and where they are in the process. The expanded page also calls out one project as a "featured project" at the top of the page.

The comments tab is self-explanatory. This is where other members may leave a comment on a specific project or the curator's work in general. Comments do not have to be completely positive, but per the Scratch Community Guidelines, any criticism should be helpful and constructive, as well as written in language suitable for public display.

The activity tab records anything that happens within a studio on any given day. A curator adding or removing a project or the name of a member who left a comment, as well as when that comment was made, are posted on an activity log.

SPEAKING OUT, HELPING OUT

When they first started creating and uploading projects in Scratch, some users were upset that their work was being remixed. After all, as the creators of projects, they felt that their work should belong only to them and not be tinkered with by others. "That led to discussions on the Web site's forums about the value of sharing and the ideas behind open-source communities," the developers wrote in a 2009 article on Scratch programming. Simply opening up the lines of communication through Scratch's online forums helped turn the tide for many concerned members, causing them to no longer to feel "ripped off" by remixes but instead proud that their work was considered worthy of others' attention.

Like comments, the Scratch forums are a way for members of the community to share their opinions and ideas. Forums are posted under several topics, new user information, the mechanics of creating a project, general information, and user interests not related to Scratch. Many of the more than fifty languages are represented in a separate forum panel, "Scratch in Other Languages."

The shared communication of the community forums has proven useful not only as a way to inform members but also as a method to help developers revise and improve the software. User suggestions and feedback posted in the forums reportedly played a key role in the development of Scratch 2.0.

JOIN THE CLUB

Beyond being members of the Scratch online community, a number of users have chosen to join communities in the physical world as well, in the form of clubs.

Even before Scratch was launched, Mitch Resnick and his team were instrumental in the creation of the Intel Computer

Mitch Resnick relaxes at MIT's Media Lab amid physical Lego bricks, rather than Scratch virtual programming bricks. Resnick had a hand in forming a popular, international network of computer clubs.

Clubhouse Network, a group of after-school centers where under-served children from low-income neighborhoods could meet to hone their computer and technology skills. The MIT Media Lab, in collaboration with Intel, got the network up and running. The first clubhouse was opened in 1993 in Boston's Computer Museum, which is part of the city's Museum of Science. The concept soon caught on outside of the greater Boston area, and by 1997, the Computer Clubhouse Network had gone international. Today, clubhouse centers are active in twenty countries worldwide. Because of the MIT Media Lab connection, Scratch is a prominent programming tool used at the centers.

In the United Kingdom, a group of volunteers established a network of Code Clubs, after-school clubs that focus on teaching computer programming to students ages nine to twelve, using Scratch. Projects are devised by organizers and guided by volunteers—primarily professional computer programmers—during one-hour

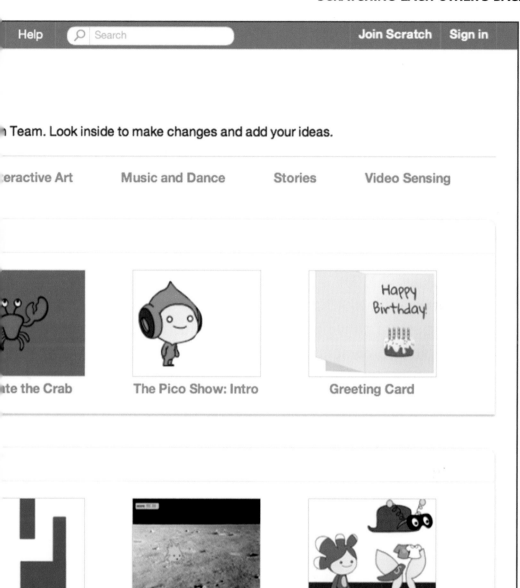

Help Search Join Scratch Sign in

Team. Look inside to make changes and add your ideas.

eractive Art   Music and Dance   Stories   Video Sensing

te the Crab   The Pico Show: Intro   Greeting Card

Happy Birthday

ze Starter   Hide and Seek   Dress Up Tera

Adapting starter projects, found on the Scratch Web site, is just one activity that can bring community members together.

sessions once a week throughout the school year. Most club sessions take place on school grounds, but some are run by, and meet in, libraries.

According to the Code Club Web site, there are more than twenty-one thousand primary schools in the United Kingdom. The organization that runs Code Club has said that it hopes to have 25 percent of those schools running a club by 2014—and eventually have a Code Club chapter in every school. Begun in 2012, Code Club was operational in more than five hundred British schools and was getting ready to start five hundred more as of February 2013.

Regardless of whether they are virtual or actual, Scratch communities are thriving around the world. Interest in simplified computer programming languages in general is growing, and Scratch is ready and able to ride that wave of success.

ATTRIBUTION The act of identifying a source or author.

BROWSER A computer program that lets users find and review information on the Internet.

BUG A trouble spot or error in a computer program, usually related to faulty code.

CLOUD A large network of computers that stores and distributes information on the Internet.

CODE A set of instructions for running a computer, written largely in strings of letters, numbers, and punctuation marks.

DOWNLOAD The act of moving information from the Internet or a large computing system to a small computing system.

INTERACTIVITY In computer science, the act of a computer program responding to actions or commands issued by a user.

INTERFACE A system that controls the way information is received and sent between a computer and a user.

METHOD A programming statement that tells objects on a computer screen how to act.

MISCHIEVOUS Capable of causing trouble in a playful manner.

NOVICE Someone who is a beginner at a task or activity.

OBJECT In programming, a collection of data stored in a computer's memory, represented as a character or other on-screen figure.

OPEN SOURCE Describing a program offered to anyone and everyone without license or fee.

PALETTE In Scratch, a rectangular area of the interface designed to hold particular categories of programming information.

PROGRAMMING The process of creating and running a set of instructions that make a computer perform certain tasks and functions.

REMIX To combine existing elements and add new ones in such a way that a new product is created.

SPRITE In Scratch, any object that appears in a user's program.

SYNTAX In programming, the rules that determine the order in which code must be placed for a program to run smoothly, or even run at all.

TINKER To make small changes to something in an attempt to fix or improve upon it.

UPLOAD To move information from a small computing system to a larger one, such as the Internet.

Association of Information Technology Professionals (AITP)
330 N. Wabash Avenue, Suite 2000
Chicago, IL 60611
(800) 224-9371
(312) 245-1070
Web site: http://www.aitp_hq@aitp.org
The Association of Information Technology Professionals, which
has gone by other names since its start in 1951, strives to
advance the information technology profession through
professional development, education, and more.

Canadian Computer Society
260 Adelaide Street East, No. 210
Toronto, ON M5A 1N1
Canada
(416) 299-5282
Web site: http://www.cancomputes.com
The Canadian Computer Society offers information, conducts
    research, and promotes study in all areas of computer
    technology.

Computing in the Core
1101 Vermont Avenue NW, Suite 400
Washington, DC 20005
(202) 349-2333
Web site: http://www.computinginthecore.org
Computing in the Core is a coalition of associations, corporations,
    scientific societies, and other nonprofits working to make

computer science education part of the K–12 core curriculum in the United States.

Educational Computing Organization of Ontario (ECOO)
10 Morrow Avenue, Suite 202
Toronto, ON M6R 2J1
Canada
(416) 538-1650
Web site: http://ecoo.org
Established in 1979, the Educational Computing Organization of
    Ontario is a nonprofit that facilitates the integration of new
    computing technology—such as Alice—into the educational
    curriculum.

HackerYou
The Centre for Social Innovation – Annex
720 Bathurst Street, Suite 500
Toronto, ON M5S 2R4
Canada
Web site: http://www.hackeryou.com
Anyone who wants to learn coding will find information, as well
as hands-on classes and workshops, through HackerYou.

Massachusetts Institute of Technology Media Lab
77 Mass. Avenue, E14/E15
Cambridge, MA 02139
Web site: http://www.media.mit.edu
The MIT Media Lab is multidisciplinary research facility focused
    on creating media-rich technology. Twenty-five research

groups, including Lifelong Kindergarten, investigate, build, and find creative uses for cutting-edge digital technologies.

National Association of Programmers (NAP)
P.O. Box 529
Prairieville, LA 70769
Web site: http://napusa.org
Formed in 1995, the National Association of Programmers is a professional organization dedicated to programmers, developers, consultants, and other professionals and students in the computer industry. It offers certification programs, conferences, and publications to its members.

WEB SITES

Due to the changing nature of Internet links, Rosen Publishing has developed an online list of Web sites related to the subject of this book. This site is updated regularly. Please use this link to access the list:

http://www.rosenlinks.com/CODE/Scrat

{FOR FURTHER READING

Badger, Michael. *Scratch 1.4: Beginner's Guide*. Birmingham, England: Packt Publishing, 2009.

Brookshear, J. Glenn. *Computer Science: An Overview*. Upper Saddle River, NJ: Prentice Hall, 2011.

Burd, Barry. *Beginning Programming with Java for Dummies*. Hoboken, NJ: Wiley, 2012.

Deane, Chris. *ICT Topics: Programming with Scratch*. Worcestershire, England: eLearning Tutors, 2012.

Farrell, Mary E. *Computer Programming for Teens*. Boston, MA: Cengage Learning PTR, 2007.

Ford, Jerry Lee, Jr. *Scratch Programming for Teens*. Boston, MA: Cengage Learning, 2008.

Gerber, Larry. *Cloud-Based Computing*. New York, NY: Rosen Classroom, 2013.

Hardnett, Charles R. *Programming Like a Pro for Teens*. Boston, MA: Cengage Learning, 2012.

Kafai, Yasmin B., et al. *The Computer Clubhouse: Constructionism and Creativity in Youth Communities*. New York, NY: Teachers College Press, 2009.

Marji, Majed. *Learn to Program with Scratch: A Visual Introduction to Programming with Art, Science, Math, and Games*. San Francisco, CA: No Starch Press, 2014.

Martinez, Sylvia Libow, and Gary S. Stager. *Invent to Learn: Making, Tinkering, and Engineering in the Classroom*. Torrance, CA: Constructing Modern Knowledge Press, 2013.

McManus, Sean. *Scratch Programming in Easy Steps*. Warwickshire, England: In Easy Steps, 2013.

Moss, Frank. *The Sorcerers and Their Apprentices: How the Digital Magicians of the MIT Media Lab Are Creating the Innovative Technologies That Will Transform Our Lives.* New York, NY: Crown Publishing, 2011.

Sande, Warren, and Carter Sande. *Hello World! Computer Programming for Kids and Other Beginners.* 2nd ed. Greenwich, CT: Manning Publications, 2013.

Shankar, Kiruba. *Copy Right & Left: Understanding Creative Commons.* Bangalore, India: Vendure Books, 2011.

Gross, Jessica. "10 Places Where Anyone Can Learn to Code."
    TED Blog, January 29, 2013. Retrieved October 2013
    (http://blog.ted.com/2013/01/29/10-places-where-anyone
    -can-learn-to-code).

Intersimone, David. "Scratch, Squeak, Alice and Go—Programming
    for Kids, Adults and Everyone Else." *Computerword*, November
    2009. Retrieved September 2013 (http://blogs.computerworld
    .com/15138/scratch_squeak_alice_and_go_programming_
    for_kids_adults_and_everyone_else).

Keshav, Karunya. "Coding, It Really Is Child's Play Now." *Hindu*,
    May 2013. Retrieved October 2013 (http://www.thehindu
    .com/sci-tech/technology/coding-it-really-is-childs-play-now/
    article4750631.ece).

Laird, Sam. "Kids Go Gaga Over Tablets." Mashable, August 29,
    2012. Retrieved October 2013 (http://mashable.com/
    2012/08/29/kids-tablets-infographic).

LEAD Project. *Scratch Super Programming Adventure*. San
    Francisco, CA; No Starch Press, 2010.

Lee, Young-Jin. "Scratch: Multimedia Programming Environment
    for Gifted Learners." *Gifted Child Today*, Spring 2011, p. 26.

Massachusetts Institute of Technology. Scratch Web site.
    Retrieved July-October 2013 (http://scratch.mit.edu).

MIT Media Lab. "Kids Coding in the Cloud." *MIT News*, May 2013.
    Retrieved October 2013 (http://web.mit.edu/newsoffice
    /2013/scratch-two-released-0514.html).

Nelson, Jennifer. "Celebrating Scratch in Libraries: Creation
    Software Helps Young People Develop 21st-Century Literacy
    Skills." *School Library Journal*, May 2009, p. 20.

Podulka, Michelle. "Just Scratching the Surface." *Learning & Leading with Technology*, February 2011, p. 32.

Resnick, Mitchel, et al. "Scratch: Programming for All." *Communications of the ACM*, November 2009, Vol. 52, No. 11, pp. 60–67.

Schorow, Stephanie. "Creating from Scratch." *MIT News*, May 2007. Retrieved October 2013 (http://web.mit.edu/news office/2007/resnick-scratch.html).

Smith, Charlotte. "New Program at South Fayette Furthers Technology Interest." TribLive.com, March 2013. Retrieved October 2013 (http://triblive.com/neighborhoods/your carlynton/yourcarlyntonmore/3612164-74/students-scratch -program#axzz2in2sPqnQ).

Solon, Olivia. "Code Club Doubles Reach, Calls for Developers to Volunteer." *Wired UK*, February 2013. Retrieved November 2013 (http://www.wired.co.uk/news/technology ?p=5&page=130).

Stross, Randall. "Computer Science for the Rest of Us." *New York Times*, April 1, 2012, Business Section, p. 5.

Wayner, Peter. "Programming for Children, Minus Cryptic Syntax." *New York Times*, November 10, 2011, p. B6.

{ INDEX

ABOUT THE AUTHOR

Jeanne Nagle is an author and editor based in upstate New York. Among the titles she has either written or edited are *Computing: From the Abacus to the iPad*, *Top STEM Careers in Technology*, *Issues in Cyberspace*, and *Careers in Internet Advertising and Marketing*.

PHOTO CREDITS

Cover © iStockphoto.com/enat; p. 5 Don Mason/Blend Images /Getty Images; p. 8 Popular Science/Getty Images; pp. 10–11 Steve Dunwell/Photolibrary/Getty Images; p. 14 Steve Liss/Time & Life Pictures/Getty Images; p. 19 Gary John Norman/Cultura/ Getty Images; pp. 22–23 Unmadindu/Wikimedia Commons/File: MIT_Media_Lab_new_building.jpg/CC BY-SA 3.0; pp. 26–27 West Coast Surfer/Getty Images; p. 31 Christophe Lehenaff /Photononstop/Getty Images; p. 36 © AP Images; p. 38 Radu Bercan/Shutterstock.com; pp. 44–45 Sami Suni/E+/Getty Images; pp. 48–49 Robert Spencer/The New York Times/Redux; pp. 50–51 Scratch is developed by the Lifelong Kindergarten Group at the MIT Media Lab. See http://scratch.mit.edu; cover and interior design elements © iStockphoto.com/letoakin (programming language), © iStockphoto.com/AF-studio (binary pattern), © iStockphoto.com/piccerella (crosshatch pattern).

Designer: Nicole Russo; Editor: Bethany Bryan;
Photo Researcher: Karen Huang